Driving Success in Manufacturing: Process Optimization for Engineering Professionals

Alfred

Copyright © [2023]

Title: Driving Success in Manufacturing: Process Optimization for Engineering Professionals
Author's: Alfred

All rights reserved. No part of this publication may be reproduced, stored in a retrieval system, or transmitted in any form or by any means, electronic, mechanical, photocopying, recording, or otherwise, without the prior written permission of the publisher or author, except in the case of brief quotations embodied in critical reviews and certain other non-commercial uses permitted by copyright law.

This book was printed and published by [Publisher's: **Alfred**] in [2023]

ISBN:

TABLE OF CONTENT

Chapter 1: Introduction to Process Optimization in Manufacturing Engineering   08

Overview of Process Optimization

Importance of Process Optimization in Manufacturing Engineering

Key Challenges in Process Optimization

Benefits of Process Optimization for Engineering Professionals

Chapter 2: Fundamentals of Manufacturing Processes   16

Types of Manufacturing Processes

Process Variables and Parameters

Key Performance Indicators in Manufacturing Processes

Role of Engineering Professionals in Manufacturing Processes

Chapter 3: Process Analysis and Evaluation   24

Data Collection and Analysis Techniques

Statistical Process Control (SPC)

Failure Mode and Effects Analysis (FMEA)

Value Stream Mapping (VSM)

Process Capability Analysis

Chapter 4: Process Optimization Techniques   34

Lean Manufacturing Principles

Six Sigma Methodology

Total Quality Management (TQM)

Just-in-Time (JIT) Manufacturing

Theory of Constraints (TOC)

Kaizen and Continuous Improvement

Chapter 5: Technology and Tools for Process Optimization   46

Automation and Robotics in Manufacturing

Computer-Aided Design and Manufacturing (CAD/CAM)

Simulation and Modeling in Process Optimization

Advanced Manufacturing Technologies

Internet of Things (IoT) in Manufacturing

Chapter 6: Implementing Process Optimization in Manufacturing Engineering   58

Creating a Culture of Continuous Improvement

Process Redesign and Reengineering

Change Management in Manufacturing Organizations

Developing Key Performance Indicators (KPIs)

Monitoring and Control Systems

Chapter 7: Case Studies in Process Optimization 69

Case Study 1: Optimizing Production Line Efficiency

Case Study 2: Reducing Manufacturing Waste and Costs

Case Study 3: Improving Quality Control Processes

Case Study 4: Enhancing Supply Chain Management

Case Study 5: Implementing Lean Principles in Manufacturing

Chapter 8: Future Trends in Process Optimization for Engineering Professionals 81

Industry 4.0 and Smart Manufacturing

Artificial Intelligence and Machine Learning in Process Optimization

Sustainability and Green Manufacturing

Advanced Analytics for Process Optimization

The Role of Engineering Professionals in the Future of Manufacturing

Chapter 9: Conclusion 92

Recap of Key Concepts

Importance of Process Optimization for Engineering Professionals

Final Thoughts and Recommendations

Chapter 1: Introduction to Process Optimization in Manufacturing Engineering

Overview of Process Optimization

In today's competitive manufacturing industry, the ability to optimize processes is crucial for engineering professionals. Process optimization plays a vital role in improving efficiency, reducing costs, and enhancing overall productivity. This subchapter provides an overview of process optimization, its key concepts, and its significance in the field of manufacturing engineering.

Process optimization can be defined as the systematic approach of improving a manufacturing process to achieve desired outcomes. It involves analyzing existing processes, identifying bottlenecks and inefficiencies, and implementing strategies to enhance performance. By optimizing processes, engineers can streamline operations, eliminate waste, and achieve higher levels of quality and productivity.

One of the fundamental concepts in process optimization is the concept of continuous improvement. Continuous improvement is a mindset that focuses on making incremental enhancements to processes over time. It involves constantly evaluating and refining processes to achieve greater efficiency and effectiveness. Engineers who embrace this concept are always seeking new methods and technologies to optimize their manufacturing processes.

Another important concept in process optimization is data-driven decision making. Engineers rely on data to identify areas for improvement and to measure the impact of process changes. By collecting and analyzing data, they can gain insights into the root causes of inefficiencies and make informed decisions to optimize their processes. This data-driven approach ensures that changes are based on evidence rather than assumptions.

Process optimization also involves the application of various tools and techniques. These tools can range from simple process mapping and value stream analysis to more complex methodologies such as Six Sigma and Lean Manufacturing. Each tool has its own purpose and can be used to address specific process optimization challenges. Engineers must have a comprehensive understanding of these tools and know how to apply them effectively in their manufacturing environment.

The significance of process optimization in manufacturing engineering cannot be overstated. It enables companies to stay competitive by improving product quality, reducing costs, and increasing customer satisfaction. By optimizing processes, engineers can identify and eliminate inefficiencies, resulting in shorter lead times and faster delivery of products to the market. Moreover, process optimization fosters innovation and encourages the adoption of new technologies, enabling companies to stay ahead in the ever-evolving manufacturing landscape.

In conclusion, process optimization is a critical aspect of manufacturing engineering. It involves continuous improvement, data-driven decision making, and the application of various tools and techniques. By optimizing processes, engineers can drive success in manufacturing by improving efficiency, reducing costs, and enhancing overall productivity.

Importance of Process Optimization in Manufacturing Engineering

Process optimization plays a crucial role in the field of manufacturing engineering. It is the key to driving success and achieving efficiency and productivity in manufacturing processes. In today's highly competitive market, manufacturers need to constantly improve their processes to stay ahead of the competition. This subchapter will delve into the importance of process optimization in manufacturing engineering and how it benefits engineers in this niche.

Process optimization involves identifying and eliminating bottlenecks, reducing waste, and enhancing overall productivity. By analyzing and improving the manufacturing processes, engineers can achieve higher quality products, reduced costs, and shorter production cycles. It enables them to make informed decisions based on data and empirical evidence rather than relying on guesswork.

One of the significant advantages of process optimization in manufacturing engineering is the ability to increase efficiency. By streamlining processes, engineers can identify areas that are consuming excessive time, energy, or resources. They can then implement strategies to eliminate or minimize these inefficiencies, resulting in improved productivity and reduced costs.

Moreover, process optimization allows engineers to identify and rectify quality issues. By analyzing the manufacturing processes, they can pinpoint areas where defects or errors are occurring and take corrective actions to prevent their recurrence. This leads to improved product quality and customer satisfaction.

Process optimization also plays a vital role in ensuring sustainability in manufacturing. By reducing waste and optimizing resource utilization, engineers can contribute to environmental conservation. This not only helps preserve the planet but also enhances a company's reputation and attracts environmentally conscious customers.

Furthermore, process optimization empowers engineers with valuable data-driven insights. By collecting and analyzing data from manufacturing processes, engineers can identify patterns, trends, and opportunities for improvement. They can then implement data-driven solutions, leading to continuous improvement and innovation.

In conclusion, process optimization is a critical aspect of manufacturing engineering. It enables engineers to streamline processes, increase efficiency, improve product quality, reduce costs, and drive success in the highly competitive manufacturing industry. By embracing process optimization techniques, engineers can stay at the forefront of technological advancements and ensure their companies remain competitive in the global market.

Key Challenges in Process Optimization

Process optimization is a crucial aspect of manufacturing engineering that aims to maximize efficiency, improve productivity, and reduce costs. However, achieving successful process optimization is not without its challenges. In this subchapter, we will explore some of the key challenges that engineers face in the pursuit of process optimization in the manufacturing industry.

One of the primary challenges in process optimization is the complexity of manufacturing systems. Today's manufacturing processes are intricate and involve numerous interconnected variables. Understanding the interdependencies between these variables and their impact on overall process performance is a daunting task. Engineers must employ advanced analytical tools and techniques to unravel the complexities and identify areas for improvement.

Another challenge lies in the availability and quality of data. Process optimization heavily relies on accurate and reliable data to make informed decisions. However, engineers often encounter challenges in collecting, organizing, and analyzing data. Incomplete or inconsistent data can lead to flawed optimization strategies and unreliable results. Engineers must invest in robust data management systems and ensure data accuracy and integrity to overcome this challenge.

Implementing process optimization initiatives also poses challenges related to resistance to change. Employees may resist changes to established processes due to fear of the unknown or the perception that their expertise is being devalued. Engineers must effectively communicate the benefits of process optimization and involve key stakeholders in the decision-making process to mitigate resistance and foster a culture of continuous improvement.

Furthermore, the rapid pace of technological advancements presents both opportunities and challenges for process optimization. While emerging technologies such as artificial intelligence, machine learning, and automation offer immense potential to streamline manufacturing processes, engineers must keep up with these advancements and adapt their skills accordingly. Failure to do so may result in a widening skills gap and hinder the successful implementation of process optimization strategies.

Lastly, financial constraints can be a significant challenge in process optimization. Implementing new technologies, conducting experiments, and hiring specialized expertise require financial resources. Engineers must develop cost-effective strategies and demonstrate the return on investment to secure necessary funding for process optimization initiatives.

In conclusion, process optimization in manufacturing engineering is a complex and challenging endeavor. Engineers must navigate the intricacies of manufacturing systems, overcome data-related obstacles, manage resistance to change, adapt to technological advancements, and address financial constraints. By understanding and addressing these challenges, engineers can drive success in manufacturing through effective process optimization strategies.

Benefits of Process Optimization for Engineering Professionals

Process optimization is a critical aspect of manufacturing engineering that aims to improve efficiency, reduce costs, and enhance overall performance. In today's highly competitive industrial landscape, engineering professionals must constantly seek ways to stay ahead of the curve and drive success in manufacturing. This subchapter explores the numerous benefits that process optimization offers to engineering professionals in the niche of manufacturing engineering.

One of the key advantages of process optimization is increased productivity. By identifying and eliminating bottlenecks, redundancies, and inefficiencies in manufacturing processes, engineers can streamline operations and boost productivity. This leads to higher output levels, shorter lead times, and improved customer satisfaction. Through process optimization, engineering professionals can maximize their resources, minimize downtime, and enhance overall operational efficiency.

Cost reduction is another significant benefit of process optimization. By optimizing manufacturing processes, engineers can identify areas of waste and implement strategies to eliminate or reduce them. This includes reducing material waste, energy consumption, and labor costs. Through process optimization, engineering professionals can identify cost-saving opportunities, such as implementing lean manufacturing principles, adopting new technologies, or automating certain tasks. This not only improves the bottom line but also enables companies to remain competitive in the market.

Process optimization also plays a crucial role in ensuring product quality and consistency. By continuously monitoring and analyzing manufacturing processes, engineers can identify potential quality issues and implement corrective actions in real-time. This helps in reducing defects, minimizing rework, and maintaining consistent product quality. Furthermore, process optimization enables engineering professionals to implement robust quality control measures, ensuring that products meet the highest standards and adhere to customer requirements.

Moreover, process optimization contributes to innovation and continuous improvement. By constantly evaluating and refining manufacturing processes, engineers can identify areas for innovation and implement new technologies or methodologies. This leads to the development of more efficient and sustainable manufacturing processes, as well as the introduction of new products or features. Process optimization encourages engineering professionals to think creatively and challenge the status quo, driving innovation and positioning companies at the forefront of the industry.

In conclusion, process optimization offers a multitude of benefits for engineering professionals in the niche of manufacturing engineering. From increased productivity and cost reduction to improved product quality and innovation, the advantages of process optimization are undeniable. By embracing process optimization principles and methodologies, engineering professionals can drive success in manufacturing, enhance competitiveness, and achieve sustainable growth.

Chapter 2: Fundamentals of Manufacturing Processes

Types of Manufacturing Processes

In the vast field of manufacturing engineering, various processes are employed to transform raw materials into finished products. Each process plays a crucial role in ensuring efficiency, productivity, and quality in the manufacturing industry. This subchapter aims to provide engineers with an overview of the different types of manufacturing processes commonly used today.

1. Casting: Casting is a manufacturing process that involves pouring molten material, such as metal or plastic, into a mold. The molten material solidifies, taking the shape of the mold, and is then removed to obtain the desired product. Casting is widely used for creating complex shapes and is particularly suitable for mass production.

2. Machining: Machining refers to the process of shaping materials by removing unwanted material using various cutting tools. It includes operations such as turning, milling, drilling, and grinding. Machining is commonly used for precision manufacturing and is ideal for creating intricate parts with tight tolerances.

3. Forming: Forming processes involve shaping materials by applying external forces. Examples of forming processes include rolling, bending, stamping, and forging. These processes are often used to create products with specific geometries, such as sheet metal components, tubes, and automotive parts.

4. Joining: Joining processes are used to combine two or more components into a single entity. Welding, soldering, brazing, and

adhesive bonding are common joining techniques. Engineers must carefully select the appropriate joining process based on factors such as material compatibility, strength requirements, and cost-effectiveness.

5. Additive Manufacturing: Also known as 3D printing, additive manufacturing involves building products layer by layer using digital designs. This innovative process has gained significant popularity in recent years due to its versatility and ability to create complex geometries with minimal material waste. Additive manufacturing is particularly useful for prototyping, customization, and low-volume production.

6. Assembly: Assembly processes involve combining multiple components to create a final product. This can include manual assembly, automated assembly lines, or robotic assembly systems. Engineers must carefully plan and optimize assembly processes to ensure efficient production and minimize errors.

Understanding the different types of manufacturing processes is essential for engineers in the field of manufacturing engineering. By selecting the most appropriate process for a specific application, engineers can optimize productivity, reduce costs, and improve the overall quality of manufactured products. Additionally, staying informed about emerging manufacturing processes, such as additive manufacturing, allows engineers to stay at the forefront of technological advancements and drive success in the ever-evolving manufacturing industry.

Process Variables and Parameters

In the realm of manufacturing engineering, understanding and controlling process variables and parameters are crucial for achieving optimal performance and driving success. These variables and parameters play a significant role in ensuring consistent product quality, improving efficiency, and reducing waste. This subchapter will delve into the fundamentals of process variables and parameters and their impact on manufacturing processes.

Process variables refer to the measurable quantities that have a direct influence on the outcome of a manufacturing process. These variables can include temperature, pressure, flow rate, pH level, viscosity, and many others. By monitoring and controlling these variables, engineers can fine-tune the manufacturing process to meet desired specifications and standards. For example, in the production of pharmaceuticals, maintaining precise temperature and pressure levels is essential to ensure the integrity and efficacy of the final product.

On the other hand, process parameters are the specific settings or values assigned to process variables, which determine how the manufacturing process will be executed. Parameters can be adjusted to optimize the performance of the process and achieve desired outcomes. Examples of process parameters include cycle time, machine speed, feed rate, tooling dimensions, and material composition. By carefully selecting and adjusting these parameters, engineers can improve production efficiency, minimize defects, and reduce production costs.

Understanding the relationship between process variables and parameters is crucial for process optimization. Engineers must conduct thorough analyses to determine the optimal range and values for each variable and parameter. This involves conducting experiments, collecting data, and employing statistical methods to identify the most influential factors and their optimal values. By systematically analyzing these variables and parameters, engineers can identify bottlenecks, implement improvements, and enhance overall process performance.

Furthermore, advancements in technology have enabled the integration of automation and real-time monitoring systems, allowing engineers to continuously monitor and control process variables and parameters. This real-time feedback loop enables quick adjustments and ensures that the manufacturing process remains within the desired range, minimizing the risk of deviations and defects.

In conclusion, process variables and parameters are vital aspects of manufacturing engineering. Understanding and controlling these variables and parameters allow engineers to optimize processes, improve efficiency, and drive success in manufacturing. By continuously monitoring, analyzing, and adjusting these factors, engineers can achieve consistent product quality, reduce waste, and enhance overall manufacturing performance.

Key Performance Indicators in Manufacturing Processes

In the world of manufacturing engineering, it is crucial to have a clear understanding of the performance of various processes in order to drive success and achieve optimal results. Key Performance Indicators (KPIs) play a vital role in this regard, providing engineers with valuable insights into the efficiency, effectiveness, and overall performance of manufacturing processes.

KPIs are measurable values that reflect the progress of an organization towards its goals. They serve as a tool to monitor and evaluate the performance of processes, enabling engineers to identify areas of improvement and make data-driven decisions. By tracking KPIs, manufacturing engineers can gain a comprehensive view of the health of their processes, enabling them to optimize operations and drive success.

One of the most important KPIs in manufacturing processes is overall equipment effectiveness (OEE). OEE is a comprehensive metric that encompasses three key elements: availability, performance, and quality. By measuring the OEE, engineers can identify the factors that contribute to equipment downtime, low performance, and poor quality, allowing them to take corrective actions and enhance overall efficiency.

Another crucial KPI is the cycle time, which refers to the time it takes to complete a process or operation. By monitoring cycle time, manufacturing engineers can identify bottlenecks, reduce lead times, and improve productivity. Additionally, cycle time can help engineers identify the impact of various factors such as equipment breakdowns, changeovers, or material shortages on the overall process.

Quality is another essential aspect of manufacturing processes, and KPIs such as defect rate and first-pass yield provide insights into the quality performance. By tracking these KPIs, engineers can identify the root causes of defects, implement corrective actions, and enhance the overall quality of the final product.

Furthermore, KPIs related to cost and resource utilization, such as labor efficiency and material waste, are critical in ensuring efficient manufacturing processes. By monitoring these KPIs, engineers can identify opportunities to reduce costs, optimize resource utilization, and improve profitability.

In conclusion, for manufacturing engineers, understanding and monitoring key performance indicators are vital for optimizing processes and driving success. By tracking metrics such as overall equipment effectiveness, cycle time, quality performance, and cost-related KPIs, engineers can identify areas for improvement, make data-driven decisions, and ultimately achieve optimal results.

Role of Engineering Professionals in Manufacturing Processes

Manufacturing processes have always been at the heart of industrial development, driving innovation and economic growth. In this subchapter, we will explore the crucial role that engineering professionals play in optimizing these processes and driving success in the manufacturing industry.

The field of manufacturing engineering encompasses a wide range of activities, from designing and developing new products to improving existing production methods. Engineering professionals in this field are responsible for ensuring the efficient and cost-effective production of goods, while maintaining high-quality standards and meeting customer demands.

One of the key responsibilities of manufacturing engineers is to design and implement production systems that maximize productivity and minimize waste. These professionals are well-versed in various manufacturing techniques and technologies, such as lean manufacturing, Six Sigma, and automated systems. By applying their expertise, they can identify bottlenecks, streamline processes, and eliminate inefficiencies, ultimately improving overall productivity and reducing costs.

Engineering professionals also play a critical role in ensuring the quality of manufactured products. They are responsible for developing and implementing quality control measures, such as statistical process control and failure mode and effects analysis. By closely monitoring production processes and conducting thorough inspections, they can identify potential defects early on and take corrective actions to prevent them from reaching the market. This not only enhances customer satisfaction but also helps maintain the reputation of the manufacturing company.

Furthermore, engineering professionals in manufacturing play a significant role in driving innovation. They are constantly exploring new materials, technologies, and manufacturing methods to improve product performance, reduce production time, and enhance sustainability. By staying up to date with the latest advancements in their field, they can introduce innovative solutions that give their companies a competitive edge in the market.

In conclusion, engineering professionals in the field of manufacturing play a vital role in optimizing processes and driving success in the industry. Their expertise in production systems, quality control, and innovation enables them to continuously improve productivity, reduce costs, and deliver high-quality products to customers. By embracing their role and leveraging their skills, engineering professionals can contribute significantly to the growth and success of the manufacturing sector.

Chapter 3: Process Analysis and Evaluation

Data Collection and Analysis Techniques

In the dynamic and ever-evolving field of manufacturing engineering, effective data collection and analysis techniques play a crucial role in driving success and process optimization. As engineers, it is imperative to employ robust methodologies to collect and analyze data to gain valuable insights, make informed decisions, and enhance overall manufacturing processes.

Data collection is the foundation of any analysis, and it involves systematically gathering information to understand various aspects of a manufacturing process. There are several techniques available to engineers for data collection, including surveys, interviews, observations, and experiments. Surveys can be conducted to gather information about employee satisfaction, product quality, or customer feedback. Interviews provide an opportunity to gain in-depth insights from key stakeholders, while observations enable engineers to directly observe and record data on the shop floor. Additionally, conducting controlled experiments can help identify cause-and-effect relationships and validate hypotheses.

Once data is collected, it is essential to employ appropriate analysis techniques to extract meaningful information. Statistical analysis is a powerful tool that enables engineers to identify patterns, trends, and correlations within the data. Techniques such as descriptive statistics, regression analysis, and hypothesis testing can provide valuable insights into process performance, identify areas for improvement, and measure the impact of process changes. With the advent of advanced analytics and machine learning algorithms, engineers can leverage predictive modeling to forecast future outcomes and optimize manufacturing processes.

To ensure accurate and reliable data collection and analysis, engineers must pay close attention to data quality. This involves ensuring that data is collected consistently, accurately, and in a timely manner. Validation techniques such as data cleaning, outlier detection, and data integrity checks should be employed to eliminate errors and inconsistencies. Data security and privacy are also of utmost importance, and engineers must adhere to ethical guidelines and industry best practices to protect sensitive information.

In conclusion, data collection and analysis techniques are indispensable for manufacturing engineers striving for process optimization and driving success. By employing robust methodologies, engineers can gather valuable insights, make informed decisions, and enhance overall manufacturing processes. With the rapid advancements in technology, engineers must stay updated with the latest tools and techniques to effectively collect, analyze, and utilize data to unlock the full potential of their manufacturing operations.

Statistical Process Control (SPC)

Statistical Process Control (SPC) is a powerful tool that plays a crucial role in driving success in manufacturing. As an engineer in the field of manufacturing engineering, understanding and implementing SPC techniques can significantly improve process optimization and ensure consistent quality standards are met.

SPC is a methodology that involves using statistical analysis to monitor and control a manufacturing process. By collecting and analyzing data, engineers can gain insights into the performance of a process, identify trends, and make data-driven decisions to improve quality and efficiency. It provides a systematic approach to identify and address variations in a manufacturing process, reducing defects and waste.

One of the key principles of SPC is understanding and controlling variation. Variation is inherent in any manufacturing process, and it can lead to defects and inconsistencies in the final product. SPC helps engineers identify the sources of variation and take corrective actions to minimize its impact. By using techniques such as control charts, engineers can monitor process parameters, detect deviations from the desired targets, and initiate corrective actions before defects occur.

Another important aspect of SPC is the concept of process capability. Process capability measures the ability of a process to consistently produce products within specified limits. By analyzing process capability indices, such as Cp and Cpk, engineers can assess whether a process is capable of meeting customer requirements. If the process capability is inadequate, engineers can use SPC tools to identify areas for improvement and implement process changes to enhance capability.

Implementing SPC requires a structured approach. Engineers need to carefully select the variables to monitor, define appropriate sampling plans, and establish control limits based on statistical analysis. SPC also involves training operators and personnel involved in the process to collect accurate data and respond to out-of-control signals effectively.

In conclusion, Statistical Process Control is a vital tool for manufacturing engineers to achieve process optimization and drive success in manufacturing. By applying SPC techniques, engineers can gain valuable insights into process performance, control variation, improve quality, and enhance process capability. SPC empowers engineers to make data-driven decisions and continuously improve manufacturing processes, leading to higher customer satisfaction, reduced costs, and increased competitiveness in the field of manufacturing engineering.

Failure Mode and Effects Analysis (FMEA)

In the realm of manufacturing engineering, where efficiency and productivity are paramount, it is crucial to identify potential failures and their effects in order to mitigate risks and ensure smooth operations. Failure Mode and Effects Analysis (FMEA) is a powerful tool that enables engineers to proactively address potential failure modes and their associated risks.

Understanding Failure Mode and Effects Analysis (FMEA) is essential for engineering professionals involved in process optimization within the manufacturing industry. This subchapter aims to provide a comprehensive overview of FMEA, its importance, and how it can be effectively utilized to drive success in manufacturing.

The primary objective of FMEA is to identify and evaluate potential failure modes in a system, process, or product. By analyzing possible failure modes, their causes, and their effects, engineers can develop proactive measures to prevent or mitigate these failures. FMEA helps to minimize the likelihood of failures occurring, reduce product defects, enhance product quality, and ultimately improve customer satisfaction.

This subchapter delves into the step-by-step process of conducting an FMEA, including the identification of failure modes, determination of their severity, likelihood of occurrence, and detectability. It also explores the concept of risk priority numbers (RPNs) and how they can be used to prioritize failure modes for corrective action.

Furthermore, this subchapter outlines the benefits of implementing FMEA in manufacturing engineering. It highlights how FMEA can support process optimization by reducing costs associated with failure, minimizing rework, and preventing production delays. It also emphasizes the importance of cross-functional collaboration in FMEA implementation, as it encourages a comprehensive analysis of potential failure modes from different perspectives.

Real-world case studies and examples are utilized throughout this subchapter to illustrate the practical application of FMEA in various manufacturing scenarios. These examples showcase how FMEA can be utilized to identify critical failure modes, develop effective preventive actions, and continuously improve processes.

By thoroughly understanding and implementing FMEA, manufacturing engineers can enhance their ability to identify and address potential failures, resulting in improved process efficiency, reduced costs, and ultimately, driving success in manufacturing.

Value Stream Mapping (VSM)

In the world of manufacturing engineering, process optimization is crucial for driving success and achieving desired outcomes. One effective tool that engineers can employ to streamline their operations is Value Stream Mapping (VSM). VSM allows engineers to visualize and analyze the flow of materials and information throughout the entire manufacturing process, identifying areas of waste and inefficiency that can be targeted for improvement.

VSM is a powerful methodology that provides a comprehensive view of the entire value stream, encompassing all the steps from raw material acquisition to the delivery of the final product to the customer. By mapping out the current state of the value stream, engineers can gain a clear understanding of how materials and information move through the process, including any bottlenecks or areas of delay. This visual representation enables them to identify areas where value is being added and areas where it is being wasted.

Once the current state of the value stream is understood, engineers can develop a future state map that outlines the ideal flow of materials and information. This future state map serves as a roadmap for process improvement, allowing engineers to implement changes that eliminate waste and streamline operations. By identifying and targeting specific areas for improvement, engineers can enhance efficiency, reduce lead times, and optimize their manufacturing processes.

Value Stream Mapping is not only a tool for process optimization but also a communication tool that promotes collaboration among different stakeholders. It allows engineers to engage with colleagues, managers, and operators, facilitating a shared understanding of the current state and the desired future state. By involving all relevant parties in the mapping process, engineers can gain valuable insights and perspectives that contribute to the successful implementation of process improvements.

In conclusion, Value Stream Mapping is a powerful methodology that empowers engineers in the field of manufacturing engineering to visualize and optimize their processes. By mapping out the current state and identifying areas of waste and inefficiency, engineers can develop a future state map that serves as a roadmap for improvement. Through collaboration and communication, engineers can streamline their operations, reduce waste, and drive success in manufacturing.

Process Capability Analysis

In the dynamic world of manufacturing, process optimization plays a crucial role in achieving success. To ensure that the manufacturing processes are efficient, reliable, and capable of producing high-quality products, engineers need to employ various analytical techniques. One such technique that holds immense significance is Process Capability Analysis.

Process Capability Analysis is a statistical method used to assess the ability of a process to meet a set of predefined specifications and customer requirements. It provides engineers with valuable insights into the performance of a manufacturing process and helps them identify areas that require improvement. By analyzing process capability, engineers can determine if a process is capable of consistently producing products within the desired specifications or if it needs adjustments.

The analysis involves two key parameters: process capability index (Cp) and process performance index (Pp). Cp measures the potential capability of a process to produce within specification limits, while Pp evaluates the actual performance of the process by considering the process average and the spread of data. These indices provide engineers with quantitative measures of how well a process is performing and if it meets the required standards.

To conduct a process capability analysis, engineers need to collect data from the manufacturing process, such as measurements or observations of product characteristics. This data is then analyzed using statistical tools to calculate Cp and Pp indices. The results obtained help engineers understand the current state of the process and its ability to produce products that meet customer expectations.

Process capability analysis offers numerous benefits to manufacturing engineers. It allows them to identify and address any process variations or deviations that may impact product quality. By understanding the capability of a process, engineers can make informed decisions regarding process adjustments, equipment modifications, or design changes to enhance product quality and reduce defects.

Furthermore, process capability analysis helps engineers set realistic and achievable process specifications, ensuring that the manufacturing process remains consistent and reliable. By continuously monitoring and analyzing process capability, engineers can implement proactive measures to prevent quality issues and reduce overall costs.

In conclusion, Process Capability Analysis is a powerful tool for manufacturing engineers. It enables them to assess the performance of manufacturing processes and make data-driven decisions to optimize process efficiency, enhance product quality, and drive success in the field of manufacturing engineering. By leveraging this technique, engineers can ensure that their manufacturing processes consistently meet customer requirements, resulting in improved customer satisfaction and a competitive edge in the industry.

Chapter 4: Process Optimization Techniques

Lean Manufacturing Principles

In the fast-paced and highly competitive world of manufacturing, engineers play a vital role in driving success and ensuring process optimization. To achieve this, it is crucial for manufacturing engineers to have a thorough understanding of lean manufacturing principles. This subchapter aims to provide engineers in the field of manufacturing engineering with an in-depth exploration of these principles, their importance, and how to effectively implement them.

Lean manufacturing is a systematic approach that focuses on minimizing waste while maximizing value for the customer. It originated from the Toyota Production System and has since become a widely adopted philosophy in various industries. Understanding and implementing lean manufacturing principles can lead to increased productivity, improved quality, reduced costs, and enhanced customer satisfaction.

The subchapter begins by introducing the concept of lean manufacturing and its evolution over time. It explains the core principles of lean manufacturing, such as identifying and eliminating waste, continuous improvement, and respect for people. Each principle is discussed in detail, providing real-world examples and case studies to illustrate their practical application.

Furthermore, the subchapter delves into the various tools and techniques used in lean manufacturing. Engineers will learn about value stream mapping, 5S methodology, just-in-time production, kanban systems, and many other lean tools that can be utilized to streamline processes and eliminate waste.

In addition to understanding the principles and tools, the subchapter emphasizes the importance of a lean culture within the organization. It explains the role of leadership in driving lean transformation and highlights the need for employee engagement and empowerment. Moreover, it provides guidance on how to develop and sustain a lean mindset among team members.

To ensure successful implementation, the subchapter also discusses common challenges and obstacles that engineers may encounter during the lean journey. It offers practical solutions and strategies to overcome these challenges while maintaining focus on continuous improvement.

By the end of this subchapter, manufacturing engineers will have a comprehensive understanding of lean manufacturing principles and how to apply them in their daily work. They will be equipped with the knowledge and tools necessary to drive success in manufacturing, optimize processes, and meet the ever-increasing demands of the industry.

Six Sigma Methodology

In the world of manufacturing engineering, process optimization is a critical factor for achieving success. To drive efficiency and improve overall productivity, engineers must be well-versed in various methodologies, and one such approach that has gained significant popularity is Six Sigma.

Six Sigma is a data-driven methodology that focuses on reducing defects and errors in a manufacturing process. By systematically analyzing and improving processes, engineers can minimize variability and achieve near-perfect efficiency levels. This subchapter will delve into the core concepts and principles of the Six Sigma methodology and its application in the field of manufacturing engineering.

The chapter will begin by introducing the origins and history of Six Sigma, highlighting its evolution from Motorola in the 1980s to its widespread adoption in various industries today. Engineers will gain a comprehensive understanding of the fundamental principles behind Six Sigma, including the DMAIC (Define, Measure, Analyze, Improve, Control) approach. Each step of the DMAIC cycle will be explained in detail, providing engineers with a practical framework to apply Six Sigma in their manufacturing processes.

Moreover, the subchapter will explore the various statistical tools and techniques used in Six Sigma, such as process mapping, control charts, and hypothesis testing. These tools are vital for engineers to identify root causes of defects, measure process performance, and make data-driven decisions for improvement.

To provide real-world context, case studies and examples from successful Six Sigma implementations in manufacturing engineering will be presented. These examples will demonstrate how organizations have achieved substantial cost savings, improved product quality, and enhanced customer satisfaction through the application of Six Sigma.

Lastly, the subchapter will discuss the importance of leadership and change management in driving Six Sigma initiatives. Engineers will learn how to create a culture of continuous improvement, engage stakeholders, and sustain the gains achieved through Six Sigma projects.

By the end of this subchapter, engineers specializing in manufacturing engineering will have a solid understanding of the Six Sigma methodology and its practical application in optimizing processes. Armed with this knowledge, they will be well-equipped to drive success in their organizations by implementing Six Sigma principles and achieving measurable improvements in efficiency and quality.

Total Quality Management (TQM)

In the ever-evolving field of manufacturing engineering, the importance of quality cannot be overstated. Meeting customer expectations and delivering products that consistently meet or exceed the highest standards is key to success in this industry. This is where Total Quality Management (TQM) comes into play.

TQM is a comprehensive approach to managing quality throughout the entire manufacturing process. It focuses on enhancing customer satisfaction by continually improving all aspects of the production process. By implementing TQM principles, manufacturing engineers can optimize productivity, reduce waste, and ultimately drive success.

One of the fundamental principles of TQM is the involvement of everyone in the organization. This means that all employees, regardless of their role or level, have a responsibility to contribute to the quality improvement efforts. By fostering a culture of collaboration and continuous improvement, TQM empowers engineers and other staff members to identify and address potential quality issues before they become major problems.

Another key aspect of TQM is the emphasis on data-driven decision-making. Engineers are encouraged to collect and analyze data at every stage of the manufacturing process. By monitoring key performance indicators (KPIs) and using statistical tools, they can identify trends, patterns, and areas for improvement. This data-driven approach allows engineers to make informed decisions and take proactive measures to enhance quality and efficiency.

Furthermore, TQM promotes a customer-centric mindset. Engineers are encouraged to understand and meet customer expectations by focusing on their needs and preferences. By incorporating customer feedback into the product design and manufacturing processes, engineers can ensure that the final products meet the highest quality standards and exceed customer expectations.

Implementing TQM requires a systematic approach that involves continuous training, process standardization, and the use of quality tools and techniques. By adopting a holistic approach to quality management, manufacturing engineers can drive success by consistently delivering products that meet or exceed customer expectations while optimizing efficiency and reducing waste.

In conclusion, Total Quality Management (TQM) is a comprehensive approach to managing quality in manufacturing engineering. It empowers engineers to optimize productivity, reduce waste, and enhance customer satisfaction. By involving everyone in the organization, emphasizing data-driven decision-making, and adopting a customer-centric mindset, TQM enables manufacturing engineers to drive success and stay ahead in today's competitive market.

Just-in-Time (JIT) Manufacturing

In the world of manufacturing engineering, efficiency and productivity are paramount. To excel in this field, engineers must constantly seek innovative ways to optimize processes and streamline operations. One such method that has revolutionized the manufacturing industry is Just-in-Time (JIT) manufacturing.

JIT is a production strategy aimed at minimizing waste and maximizing efficiency. It focuses on delivering the right quantity of products at the right time, thereby reducing inventory costs and eliminating unnecessary storage. By implementing JIT, engineers can ensure that materials and components arrive precisely when they are needed, reducing lead times and improving customer satisfaction.

The concept of JIT manufacturing originated in Japan in the 1970s, with Toyota being one of its pioneers. It was a response to the need for leaner production systems that could adapt quickly to changing market demands. Today, JIT has become a cornerstone of modern manufacturing, helping companies of all sizes optimize their operations.

One of the key principles of JIT is the elimination of waste. Waste can manifest in various forms, such as excess inventory, overproduction, defects, and unnecessary transportation. By identifying and eliminating these inefficiencies, engineers can significantly reduce costs and improve overall productivity.

To implement JIT successfully, engineers must focus on several critical areas. First and foremost, they need to establish strong relationships with suppliers to ensure timely delivery of materials. This involves working closely with suppliers, monitoring their performance, and developing contingency plans to mitigate any potential disruptions.

Secondly, engineers must carefully analyze and optimize the production process. They need to identify bottlenecks, minimize setup times, and continuously improve workflow to achieve smooth and seamless operations. This requires a deep understanding of the entire production chain and the ability to leverage technology and automation whenever possible.

Furthermore, communication plays a vital role in JIT manufacturing. Engineers must foster effective collaboration between different departments, such as supply chain, logistics, and quality control, to ensure a synchronized and well-coordinated operation. Regular feedback loops and open lines of communication are essential to address any issues promptly and make necessary adjustments.

In conclusion, Just-in-Time (JIT) manufacturing is a powerful strategy that can drive success in the field of manufacturing engineering. By adopting JIT principles, engineers can eliminate waste, reduce costs, and improve efficiency. However, implementing JIT requires a holistic approach, encompassing supplier relationships, process optimization, and effective communication. With the right tools and mindset, engineers can leverage JIT to optimize manufacturing processes and stay ahead in the competitive manufacturing industry.

Theory of Constraints (TOC)

In the world of manufacturing engineering, optimizing processes to drive success is crucial. To achieve this, engineers need to have a deep understanding of various methodologies and tools. One such methodology that has proven to be highly effective is the Theory of Constraints (TOC). In this subchapter, we will delve into the intricacies of TOC and its significance in the realm of manufacturing.

The Theory of Constraints is a management philosophy that focuses on identifying and eliminating bottlenecks or constraints in a system to improve overall efficiency. It was introduced by Dr. Eliyahu M. Goldratt in his book "The Goal" and has since gained immense popularity among manufacturing professionals.

TOC operates on the premise that every system, whether it's a manufacturing process or an entire supply chain, has at least one constraint that limits its overall performance. By identifying and resolving these constraints, engineers can enhance productivity, reduce cycle times, and increase throughput.

The first step in implementing TOC is to identify the constraint or bottleneck. This can be a machine, a process, or even a specific resource. Once identified, engineers can then focus their efforts on optimizing the constraint to increase its capacity. This may involve employing techniques such as reducing setup times, improving maintenance procedures, or increasing the availability of the bottleneck resource.

However, TOC goes beyond just optimizing the constraint. It emphasizes the importance of synchronizing the entire system to ensure smooth flow and minimize the negative impact of the constraint on other processes. This requires engineers to carefully manage the flow of materials, information, and resources throughout the system, ensuring that the constraint is utilized to its maximum potential.

TOC also stresses the significance of measurements and performance indicators to monitor the system's progress. Engineers need to establish relevant metrics that track the constraint's performance and its impact on the overall system. By continuously monitoring these metrics, they can identify potential issues and take corrective actions promptly.

In conclusion, the Theory of Constraints is a powerful tool for engineers in the field of manufacturing engineering. By identifying and optimizing constraints, synchronizing the system, and monitoring performance, engineers can drive success and achieve remarkable improvements in productivity, efficiency, and overall operational performance. By incorporating TOC into their arsenal of methodologies, manufacturing engineers can unlock the full potential of their processes and propel their organizations to new heights of success.

Kaizen and Continuous Improvement

In the world of manufacturing engineering, the pursuit of excellence and efficiency is an ever-present goal. To remain competitive in today's market, companies must constantly evolve and improve their processes. This subchapter explores the concept of Kaizen and how it can drive continuous improvement in manufacturing operations.

Kaizen, a Japanese term meaning "continuous improvement," is a philosophy that encourages small, incremental changes in processes, products, and systems. It emphasizes the involvement of all employees in identifying and implementing improvements, fostering a culture of continuous learning and growth.

The subchapter begins by delving into the history and principles of Kaizen. It highlights how Kaizen originated from the Toyota Production System and became a cornerstone of Japanese manufacturing success. The principles of Kaizen, including standardization, waste reduction, and employee empowerment, are discussed in detail, showcasing the relevance and applicability of these principles in modern manufacturing engineering.

Next, the subchapter explores the various tools and techniques used in Kaizen. It introduces methods such as value stream mapping, 5S, Kanban, and Poka-Yoke, explaining how these tools can be applied to identify inefficiencies, eliminate waste, and streamline processes. Real-life case studies and examples from different manufacturing industries provide practical insights into the successful implementation of these techniques.

Moreover, the subchapter emphasizes the role of engineers in driving Kaizen initiatives. It highlights the importance of engineering professionals in analyzing data, identifying bottlenecks, and proposing innovative solutions. It also addresses the challenges engineers may face during the implementation process and offers strategies to overcome them.

Furthermore, the subchapter discusses the benefits of Kaizen and continuous improvement in manufacturing engineering. It emphasizes how adopting Kaizen principles can lead to improved quality, increased productivity, reduced costs, and enhanced employee morale. The chapter also explores the role of technology, such as automation and data analytics, in supporting continuous improvement efforts.

Finally, the subchapter concludes with a call to action for engineers in the manufacturing industry. It encourages them to embrace the philosophy of Kaizen, engage in continuous learning and improvement, and become catalysts for change within their organizations. By doing so, engineers can drive success in manufacturing and contribute to the overall growth and competitiveness of their companies.

Overall, this subchapter provides a comprehensive overview of Kaizen and continuous improvement in manufacturing engineering. It equips engineers with the knowledge and tools necessary to implement and sustain a culture of continuous improvement within their organizations.

Chapter 5: Technology and Tools for Process Optimization

Automation and Robotics in Manufacturing

In recent years, the manufacturing industry has witnessed a significant transformation due to the rapid advancements in automation and robotics technology. This subchapter explores the various ways in which automation and robotics have revolutionized the field of manufacturing engineering, enabling organizations to drive success and achieve process optimization.

Automation refers to the use of computer software or machinery to perform tasks with minimal human intervention. It has become an integral part of manufacturing operations, offering numerous benefits to engineers and organizations alike. By automating repetitive and mundane tasks, engineers can focus on more complex and strategic activities, leading to increased productivity and efficiency.

Robotics, on the other hand, involves the use of automated machines, known as robots, to perform tasks traditionally carried out by humans. These robots are equipped with advanced sensors and artificial intelligence capabilities, enabling them to operate autonomously and adapt to changing environments. By leveraging robotics technology, manufacturing engineers can accelerate production processes, improve product quality, and enhance workplace safety.

One of the key advantages of automation and robotics in manufacturing is the ability to achieve higher levels of precision and accuracy. Robots can perform intricate tasks with unparalleled precision, resulting in consistent product quality and reduced error rates. This level of precision is particularly crucial in industries such as aerospace, automotive, and electronics, where even the slightest deviation can have significant consequences.

Furthermore, automation and robotics enable manufacturing engineers to streamline production processes and optimize resource utilization. By integrating automated systems into the manufacturing line, engineers can eliminate bottlenecks, reduce cycle times, and increase throughput. This leads to improved operational efficiency and cost savings, allowing organizations to stay competitive in the global market.

Additionally, automation and robotics have revolutionized workplace safety in the manufacturing industry. By deploying robots to perform hazardous tasks, engineers can minimize the risk of accidents and injuries. This not only protects the well-being of workers but also mitigates potential legal and financial liabilities for organizations.

However, the adoption of automation and robotics in manufacturing does come with its challenges. Engineers need to possess a deep understanding of these technologies and be skilled in their implementation. Furthermore, organizations must invest in appropriate training programs to equip their workforce with the necessary skills to operate and maintain automated systems.

In conclusion, automation and robotics have transformed the manufacturing industry, offering numerous benefits to engineers and organizations. By leveraging these technologies, manufacturing engineers can achieve process optimization, improve product quality, enhance workplace safety, and drive success in a highly competitive market. It is imperative for engineering professionals in the field of manufacturing engineering to stay updated with the latest advancements in automation and robotics to effectively harness their potential and stay ahead of the curve.

Computer-Aided Design and Manufacturing (CAD/CAM)

In today's fast-paced and competitive manufacturing industry, engineers play a crucial role in driving success. With the advent of technology, one of the most significant advancements in the field of manufacturing engineering has been the integration of Computer-Aided Design and Manufacturing (CAD/CAM) systems. This subchapter explores the transformative power of CAD/CAM and its impact on process optimization for engineering professionals.

CAD/CAM combines the power of computer software and hardware to streamline the design and manufacturing processes. It enables engineers to create, modify, and analyze designs with unparalleled precision and efficiency. By using CAD software, engineers can visualize their ideas in 2D or 3D models, allowing for a more comprehensive understanding of the product. This visualization aids in identifying design flaws, optimizing designs, and improving functionality.

Moreover, CAD/CAM systems facilitate seamless communication between different departments involved in the manufacturing process. Engineers can collaborate with other professionals, such as designers, machinists, and quality control experts, to ensure that designs are manufacturable and meet the desired specifications. This collaboration reduces errors and minimizes the need for rework, resulting in significant time and cost savings.

CAM software, on the other hand, takes the design created in CAD and translates it into machine instructions for manufacturing. By automating the manufacturing process, CAM eliminates human errors while maximizing efficiency. It enables engineers to generate tool paths, simulate machining operations, and optimize cutting parameters, leading to improved productivity and shorter lead times.

The integration of CAD/CAM systems also opens up new possibilities for advanced manufacturing techniques, such as additive manufacturing (3D printing) and computer numerical control (CNC) machining. These technologies allow engineers to create complex geometries, reduce material waste, and achieve high levels of precision. CAD/CAM systems are indispensable in harnessing the full potential of these cutting-edge manufacturing methods.

In conclusion, CAD/CAM systems have revolutionized the field of manufacturing engineering. By providing engineers with powerful tools for design visualization, collaboration, and process automation, CAD/CAM has become an essential component of process optimization. Manufacturing professionals who leverage the capabilities of CAD/CAM can drive success by reducing errors, improving productivity, and embracing advanced manufacturing technologies. As the manufacturing industry continues to evolve, engineers must stay abreast of the latest CAD/CAM advancements to remain competitive in their respective niches.

Simulation and Modeling in Process Optimization

In the ever-evolving field of manufacturing engineering, process optimization plays a crucial role in improving productivity, efficiency, and overall success. One of the most powerful tools available to engineers in this pursuit is simulation and modeling. This subchapter will explore the significance of simulation and modeling in process optimization and how they can drive success in the manufacturing industry.

Simulation involves creating a virtual representation of a real-world system or process. By mimicking the behavior of the actual system, engineers can gain insights into its performance and identify areas for improvement. In the context of process optimization, simulation allows engineers to experiment with various scenarios and evaluate their impact on key performance indicators.

Modeling, on the other hand, involves creating mathematical or statistical representations of a system. These models can help engineers understand complex relationships between variables and predict outcomes. By utilizing models, engineers can make informed decisions and devise strategies to optimize processes.

Simulation and modeling offer several advantages in the realm of process optimization. Firstly, they provide a safe and cost-effective environment for testing and experimentation. Instead of conducting physical trials that may be time-consuming and expensive, engineers can simulate different process configurations and evaluate their effectiveness virtually. This ability to quickly iterate and analyze multiple scenarios accelerates the optimization process significantly.

Furthermore, simulation and modeling enable engineers to identify bottlenecks, inefficiencies, and potential risks within a manufacturing process. By visualizing and analyzing the simulated system, engineers can pinpoint areas that require improvement and develop strategies to address them effectively. This proactive approach minimizes the chances of costly errors and ensures that the optimized process is robust and reliable.

In addition to process optimization, simulation and modeling also contribute to innovation in manufacturing. Engineers can leverage these tools to explore new ideas, technologies, and concepts before implementing them in the real world. This ability to experiment in a virtual environment fosters creativity and enables engineers to push the boundaries of what is possible in manufacturing.

In conclusion, simulation and modeling are indispensable tools for engineers in the niche of manufacturing engineering. By utilizing these tools, engineers can optimize processes, improve productivity, and drive success in the manufacturing industry. Simulation and modeling offer a safe and cost-effective way to test and experiment, identify inefficiencies, and promote innovation. Embracing simulation and modeling as part of the process optimization journey is essential for engineering professionals seeking to stay ahead in the competitive landscape of manufacturing.

Advanced Manufacturing Technologies

In today's rapidly evolving world, the field of manufacturing engineering is no exception to the constant technological advancements. To stay competitive and drive success, engineers need to keep up with the latest manufacturing technologies. This subchapter, titled "Advanced Manufacturing Technologies," aims to provide engineers in the manufacturing engineering niche with valuable insights into the cutting-edge technologies that are shaping the industry.

1. Introduction to Advanced Manufacturing Technologies
In this section, we will discuss the importance of embracing advanced manufacturing technologies in the current market landscape. We will explore how these technologies can improve productivity, efficiency, and overall product quality, leading to a competitive advantage for manufacturers.

2. Additive Manufacturing (3D Printing)
Additive manufacturing, also known as 3D printing, has revolutionized the manufacturing industry. We will delve into the various additive manufacturing techniques, such as selective laser sintering and fused deposition modeling, and their applications across different sectors. Engineers will learn about the benefits and challenges of adopting 3D printing and how it can transform traditional manufacturing processes.

3. Robotics and Automation
Robots and automation have become integral to modern manufacturing plants. This section will explore the role of robotics in

assembly lines, material handling, and quality control. Engineers will gain insights into the latest advancements in robotic technologies, including collaborative robots (cobots) and artificial intelligence (AI)-powered systems.

4. Internet of Things (IoT) and Industrial Internet of Things (IIoT)
The IoT and IIoT have enabled a seamless connection between machines, devices, and systems, leading to smart factories. Here, engineers will discover how IoT and IIoT technologies can enhance process optimization, predictive maintenance, and real-time data analytics, ultimately enabling faster decision-making and improved operational efficiency.

5. Augmented Reality (AR) and Virtual Reality (VR)
AR and VR have found applications in training, design, and simulation within manufacturing environments. This section will explore how engineers can leverage these technologies to streamline product development, reduce design errors, and enhance training programs, resulting in cost savings and improved productivity.

6. Advanced Materials and Nanotechnology
Advanced materials and nanotechnology are driving innovation in manufacturing. This part will discuss the latest breakthroughs in materials science, such as carbon nanotubes, graphene, and smart materials. Engineers will gain insights into how these advanced materials can improve product performance, durability, and sustainability.

7. Future Trends and Challenges
The subchapter concludes by discussing the future trends and

challenges in advanced manufacturing technologies. Engineers will be encouraged to embrace a mindset of continuous learning and adaptability to stay ahead in this dynamic industry.

By exploring the various advanced manufacturing technologies covered in this subchapter, engineers in the manufacturing engineering niche will be equipped with the knowledge and tools necessary to drive success in their respective fields. Embracing these technologies will not only enhance productivity and efficiency but also position manufacturers at the forefront of innovation in an increasingly competitive global market.

Internet of Things (IoT) in Manufacturing

The Internet of Things (IoT) has revolutionized various industries, and manufacturing is no exception. In recent years, IoT adoption in manufacturing engineering has gained significant momentum, transforming traditional manufacturing processes into highly efficient and automated systems. This subchapter will delve into the role of IoT in manufacturing, its benefits, and its impact on the field of manufacturing engineering.

IoT in manufacturing refers to the integration of sensors, devices, and software systems that connect and communicate with each other to collect and exchange data. This interconnected network enables real-time monitoring, analysis, and control of manufacturing operations, leading to increased productivity, improved quality, and reduced costs.

One of the key benefits of IoT in manufacturing is predictive maintenance. By leveraging IoT sensors, manufacturers can monitor the health of machinery and equipment in real-time, detecting potential issues before they cause major breakdowns. This proactive approach to maintenance not only minimizes downtime but also prolongs the lifespan of machinery, ultimately improving overall operational efficiency.

Additionally, IoT facilitates the concept of the smart factory, where machines, processes, and humans work in perfect harmony. Through IoT-enabled solutions, manufacturers can automate various aspects of the production line, such as inventory management, supply chain optimization, and quality control. This automation not only reduces human error but also streamlines operations, leading to faster production cycles and increased output.

Furthermore, IoT in manufacturing opens up new possibilities for data analytics and machine learning. The vast amount of data collected from IoT sensors can be analyzed to identify patterns, trends, and anomalies. This data-driven approach enables manufacturers to make informed decisions, optimize processes, and even predict future market demands, giving them a competitive edge in the industry.

However, with the integration of IoT in manufacturing comes the challenge of ensuring data security and privacy. As more devices and systems become interconnected, manufacturers must implement robust cybersecurity measures to protect sensitive information and prevent unauthorized access.

In conclusion, IoT has transformed the landscape of manufacturing engineering, offering unprecedented opportunities for optimization and automation. By leveraging IoT technologies, engineers in the manufacturing industry can streamline processes, reduce costs, and improve overall operational efficiency. However, it is crucial to address security concerns and implement robust cybersecurity measures to safeguard data and maintain the trust of customers and stakeholders. The future of manufacturing lies in the seamless integration of IoT, enabling a new era of smart factories and data-driven decision making.

Chapter 6: Implementing Process Optimization in Manufacturing Engineering

Creating a Culture of Continuous Improvement

In the fast-paced and highly competitive world of manufacturing engineering, the ability to adapt and continuously improve is crucial for success. To stay ahead of the competition, engineers must foster a culture of continuous improvement within their organizations. This subchapter delves into the key strategies and best practices for creating such a culture, enabling manufacturing professionals to optimize their processes and drive success.

1. Emphasize the Importance of Continuous Improvement: Engineers must educate their teams about the significance of continuous improvement. By explaining how small, incremental changes can lead to significant improvements in quality, efficiency, and profitability, they can inspire their colleagues to embrace this mindset.

2. Empower Employees: Encourage all employees, from the shop floor to the management level, to actively participate in the improvement process. Provide them with the necessary tools, resources, and training to identify and implement innovative ideas. Recognize and reward employees who contribute to the ongoing improvement efforts, fostering a sense of ownership and motivation.

3. Foster Collaboration and Knowledge Sharing: Establish a culture that promotes open communication and collaboration among team members. Encourage regular meetings, brainstorming sessions, and cross-functional collaborations to share best practices, lessons learned,

and innovative ideas. By pooling their expertise and experiences, engineers can identify improvement opportunities and implement effective solutions.

4. Implement Lean Manufacturing Principles: Adopting lean manufacturing principles, such as just-in-time production, waste reduction, and continuous flow, can significantly improve efficiency and productivity. Engineers should educate themselves and their teams about lean methodologies and facilitate their implementation throughout the manufacturing process.

5. Implement Data-Driven Decision Making: Encourage engineers to collect and analyze data to drive informed decision-making. Implementing data tracking systems, such as key performance indicators (KPIs), allows for real-time monitoring of production processes, enabling quick identification of areas for improvement. Regularly review and analyze the data to identify trends, patterns, and potential bottlenecks, facilitating data-driven decision-making.

6. Encourage a Learning Culture: Engineers should foster a learning culture within their organizations, encouraging employees to pursue professional development opportunities. By investing in training programs and certifications, engineers can enhance their skills and knowledge, contributing to the overall improvement efforts of the organization.

By implementing these strategies and best practices, engineers can create a culture of continuous improvement within their manufacturing organizations. This culture will empower employees, encourage collaboration, and drive the adoption of innovative ideas and lean methodologies. Ultimately, this will lead to optimized processes, increased efficiency, improved quality, and sustained success in the competitive manufacturing engineering industry.

Process Redesign and Reengineering

In today's fast-paced manufacturing industry, engineers play a crucial role in driving success and ensuring optimal process efficiency. As manufacturing engineering professionals, it is essential to constantly evaluate and improve existing processes to stay ahead of the competition and meet ever-changing customer demands. This subchapter aims to delve into the concepts of process redesign and reengineering, providing engineers with valuable insights and strategies to optimize their manufacturing processes.

Process redesign involves taking a step back from existing processes and critically evaluating their effectiveness. It requires engineers to identify areas of improvement and implement changes that enhance overall efficiency, reduce costs, and increase productivity. By thoroughly analyzing each step in the manufacturing process, engineers can identify bottlenecks, eliminate redundancies, and streamline operations for maximum output.

Reengineering, on the other hand, takes process redesign a step further by challenging traditional methodologies and embracing innovative approaches. It involves radical changes that completely transform the way manufacturing processes are designed and executed. Reengineering enables engineers to think outside the box, leverage emerging technologies, and create new, efficient ways of producing goods.

To successfully undertake process redesign and reengineering, engineers must first understand the goals and objectives of their organization. By aligning process optimization efforts with business objectives, engineers can ensure that any changes made directly contribute to achieving overarching strategic goals.

Furthermore, engineers must involve cross-functional teams in the process redesign and reengineering initiatives. This collaborative approach brings together individuals from various departments, leveraging their expertise and diverse perspectives to identify areas for improvement. By fostering a culture of continuous improvement, engineers can create an environment that encourages innovation and drives success.

It is also crucial for engineers to leverage cutting-edge technologies and tools to support process redesign and reengineering efforts. Automation, data analytics, and machine learning can provide valuable insights and help engineers identify patterns, inefficiencies, and opportunities for optimization. By leveraging these technologies, engineers can make informed decisions and implement changes that yield tangible results.

In summary, process redesign and reengineering are essential aspects of manufacturing engineering. By continuously evaluating and improving existing processes, engineers can drive success, increase efficiency, and remain competitive in the dynamic manufacturing industry. By embracing innovative approaches, involving cross-functional teams, and leveraging modern technologies, engineers can optimize their manufacturing processes and deliver exceptional results.

Change Management in Manufacturing Organizations

As manufacturing engineers, we understand the critical role that change plays in our industry. The ability to adapt and evolve is essential for driving success in manufacturing organizations. However, implementing change can be a complex process that requires careful planning, communication, and execution. In this subchapter, we will explore the concept of change management and its significance in manufacturing organizations.

Change management refers to the structured approach of transitioning individuals, teams, and organizations from a current state to a desired future state. It involves identifying the need for change, creating a strategy, and effectively implementing and sustaining the change. In the context of manufacturing organizations, change management is crucial for optimizing processes, improving efficiency, and staying competitive in a rapidly evolving industry.

One of the key challenges in change management is resistance to change. People tend to be comfortable with familiar routines and processes, and introducing new ways of doing things can be met with resistance. Therefore, effective change management requires addressing and managing this resistance through open communication, involvement, and training. It is important to engage all stakeholders, including employees, managers, and executives, in the change process to ensure their buy-in and commitment.

In manufacturing organizations, change management often encompasses various aspects, such as implementing new technologies, adopting lean manufacturing principles, or reorganizing production lines. Regardless of the specific change, a structured approach is essential. This includes conducting a thorough analysis of the current state, defining the desired future state, and developing a comprehensive plan for achieving the desired outcomes.

Furthermore, change management should not be a one-time event but an ongoing process. Continuous improvement is a fundamental principle in manufacturing, and change management plays a crucial role in driving and sustaining this improvement. Regularly evaluating and monitoring the implemented changes, gathering feedback from employees, and making necessary adjustments are essential for long-term success.

In conclusion, change management is a critical component of driving success in manufacturing organizations. As manufacturing engineers, we must embrace change and understand the significance of effectively managing it. By adopting a structured approach, addressing resistance, and ensuring ongoing improvement, we can optimize processes, improve efficiency, and stay competitive in the ever-evolving manufacturing industry.

Developing Key Performance Indicators (KPIs)

Key Performance Indicators (KPIs) play a crucial role in driving success in the field of manufacturing engineering. KPIs are quantifiable metrics that measure the performance of various processes and activities within a manufacturing organization. By tracking and analyzing these indicators, engineers can gain valuable insights into the efficiency, effectiveness, and overall performance of their manufacturing operations.

In this subchapter, we will explore the process of developing KPIs that are specifically tailored for the manufacturing engineering niche. Whether you are working in a large-scale production facility or a smaller manufacturing operation, understanding the principles of KPI development is essential for optimizing processes and driving continuous improvement.

The first step in developing KPIs is to identify the specific goals and objectives of your manufacturing operation. What are the key areas that you want to measure and improve? These could include quality control, production efficiency, cost reduction, or employee productivity. By clearly defining your goals, you can align your KPIs with your overall business objectives.

Next, you need to determine the most relevant metrics for measuring performance in each area. For example, in quality control, you may want to track metrics such as defect rate, customer complaints, or product rework. In production efficiency, you might consider metrics like cycle time, machine downtime, or overall equipment effectiveness

(OEE). It is important to select metrics that are meaningful, measurable, and aligned with your goals.

Once you have identified the relevant metrics, you can establish targets or benchmarks for each KPI. These targets should be realistic, achievable, and based on historical data or industry standards. Setting targets will help you monitor progress and identify areas that require improvement.

To effectively measure and track KPIs, it is crucial to establish a robust data collection and reporting system. This may involve implementing software solutions, utilizing data analytics tools, or developing custom reporting templates. Regularly reviewing and analyzing the data will provide you with insights into performance trends, areas of concern, and opportunities for optimization.

In conclusion, developing KPIs is a vital process for engineers in the manufacturing engineering niche. By carefully selecting and tracking relevant metrics, engineers can gain visibility into their manufacturing operations, identify areas for improvement, and drive success. Implementing a systematic approach to KPI development will enable manufacturing professionals to optimize processes, enhance productivity, and achieve their business objectives.

Monitoring and Control Systems

In today's highly competitive manufacturing industry, the ability to monitor and control various processes is crucial for achieving optimal efficiency and ensuring the highest quality standards. Monitoring and control systems play a vital role in enabling engineers to identify and rectify any deviations or issues that may arise during the manufacturing process. This subchapter aims to provide engineers in the field of manufacturing engineering with a comprehensive understanding of monitoring and control systems and their significance in driving success in manufacturing.

The subchapter begins by introducing the concept of monitoring and control systems, highlighting their purpose and the benefits they offer. It emphasizes the need for real-time data collection and analysis to facilitate informed decision-making and process improvements. By implementing robust monitoring and control systems, engineers can gain valuable insights into the performance of various manufacturing processes, enabling them to identify bottlenecks, inefficiencies, and potential areas for optimization.

Next, the subchapter delves into the different types of monitoring and control systems commonly used in manufacturing engineering. It explores the role of supervisory control and data acquisition (SCADA) systems, which enable engineers to remotely monitor and control multiple processes simultaneously. It also discusses the importance of distributed control systems (DCS) and their ability to provide centralized control and monitoring of complex manufacturing operations.

Furthermore, the subchapter explores the various sensors and instruments employed in monitoring and control systems, such as pressure sensors, temperature sensors, flow meters, and level detectors. It elucidates their functions and applications in different manufacturing processes, stressing the importance of choosing the right sensors for accurate data collection.

The subchapter also touches upon the integration of monitoring and control systems with emerging technologies such as the Internet of Things (IoT) and artificial intelligence (AI). It discusses how these technologies can enhance the capabilities of monitoring and control systems, enabling engineers to predict and prevent potential issues, optimize processes, and achieve higher levels of automation.

To conclude, this subchapter emphasizes the critical role of monitoring and control systems in driving success in manufacturing engineering. By implementing robust systems and leveraging advanced technologies, engineers can optimize processes, improve product quality, reduce waste, and enhance overall operational efficiency. With an in-depth understanding of monitoring and control systems, manufacturing engineers can stay at the forefront of the industry and contribute to the success of their organizations.

Chapter 7: Case Studies in Process Optimization

Case Study 1: Optimizing Production Line Efficiency

Introduction:

In the highly competitive world of manufacturing, process optimization plays a crucial role in driving success and maintaining a competitive edge. This subchapter presents a real-life case study that highlights how engineers in the field of manufacturing engineering can enhance production line efficiency through effective process optimization techniques.

Background:

The manufacturing industry constantly faces challenges to improve productivity, reduce costs, and meet customer demands. This case study focuses on a company that specializes in the production of automotive components. The company was struggling with low production line efficiency, resulting in increased costs and delayed deliveries.

Challenges Faced:

1. Bottlenecks: The production line experienced bottlenecks at certain stages, causing delays and hampering overall efficiency.
2. Inefficient Layout: The factory layout did not support a smooth workflow, leading to unnecessary movement of materials and equipment, causing delays and inefficiencies.
3. Lack of Standardization: Processes were not standardized, leading to inconsistencies, quality issues, and time wastage.

Steps Taken:

1. Data Collection: Engineers conducted a detailed analysis of the existing processes, collecting data on production rates, downtime, and bottlenecks. This data formed the foundation for process optimization.

2. Value Stream Mapping: By creating a visual representation of the production process, engineers identified areas of improvement and waste reduction opportunities. This helped them to streamline operations and eliminate non-value-added activities.

3. Layout Optimization: The engineers redesigned the factory layout, ensuring a more logical flow of materials and equipment. This minimized unnecessary movement, reduced production time, and improved overall efficiency.

4. Standardization: To eliminate inconsistencies and improve quality, engineers implemented standard operating procedures (SOPs) and trained employees accordingly. This ensured that everyone followed the same processes, resulting in improved efficiency and reduced errors.

Results and Benefits:

The implementation of process optimization techniques led to significant improvements in production line efficiency for the automotive component manufacturer. The bottlenecks were eliminated, and the production rate increased by 20%. The optimized factory layout reduced material movement by 30%, resulting in reduced downtime and improved productivity. Moreover, the standardization of processes improved quality, reduced errors, and minimized rework, leading to enhanced customer satisfaction.

Conclusion:

This case study demonstrates the importance of process optimization in manufacturing engineering. By analyzing data, streamlining operations, optimizing layouts, and implementing standardization, engineers can significantly enhance production line efficiency, reduce costs, and meet customer demands. Process optimization is a key driver of success in the manufacturing industry, and engineers must embrace it as an essential tool in their toolbox.

Case Study 2: Reducing Manufacturing Waste and Costs

In this case study, we will explore a real-life example of how a manufacturing company successfully reduced waste and costs through process optimization. By implementing innovative strategies and leveraging engineering expertise, the company was able to drive success and achieve remarkable results.

The manufacturing industry is constantly challenged to find ways to improve efficiency, reduce waste, and cut costs. This case study highlights the importance of continuous improvement and the role engineers play in driving success in manufacturing.

The company in focus is a leading player in the manufacturing engineering niche. They were facing significant challenges related to waste generation and rising costs. In order to address these issues, the company formed a cross-functional team consisting of engineers from various disciplines.

The team began by conducting a detailed analysis of the existing manufacturing processes. By closely examining each step, they identified areas where waste was being generated and costs were escalating. This analysis allowed them to pinpoint key bottlenecks and inefficiencies.

Next, the team brainstormed innovative solutions to tackle the identified challenges. Through collaborative efforts, they developed alternative processes and technologies that would help reduce waste, streamline production, and cut costs. These solutions were carefully evaluated, taking into account their feasibility, impact, and potential risks.

Once the solutions were finalized, the team proceeded with implementation. They worked closely with production personnel to ensure a smooth transition and minimize disruptions. The engineers played a crucial role in overseeing the implementation, monitoring progress, and making necessary adjustments along the way.

The results were astounding. Through the optimized processes, the company was able to reduce waste generation by 30% and cut costs by 20%. These improvements not only had a positive impact on the bottom line but also contributed to the company's sustainability goals.

This case study serves as a testament to the power of process optimization and the valuable contributions engineers can make in the manufacturing industry. By leveraging their expertise, engineers can identify inefficiencies, develop innovative solutions, and drive success in manufacturing.

In conclusion, reducing manufacturing waste and costs is a critical objective for manufacturing companies. This case study highlights the importance of process optimization and the pivotal role engineers play in achieving such goals. By continuously seeking improvement and leveraging their expertise, engineers can help manufacturing companies thrive in a competitive landscape while also contributing to environmental sustainability.

Case Study 3: Improving Quality Control Processes

In today's competitive manufacturing industry, delivering high-quality products is crucial for success. As manufacturing engineers, you play a pivotal role in ensuring that quality control processes are optimized to meet customer expectations and industry standards. This case study will explore a real-world example of how a company improved its quality control processes, resulting in enhanced product quality and customer satisfaction.

The Problem:

Company XYZ, a leading manufacturer of electronic components, was facing a significant challenge with its quality control processes. Despite having well-established quality control procedures in place, they were experiencing an increasing number of customer complaints regarding product defects. This issue not only affected their reputation but also resulted in substantial financial losses due to product recalls and warranty claims. The company recognized the urgent need to address this problem and sought the expertise of its manufacturing engineering team.

The Solution:

The manufacturing engineering team embarked on a comprehensive analysis of the existing quality control processes to identify areas of improvement. They utilized statistical process control techniques to identify patterns and trends in the defect data. This analysis revealed that a significant number of defects were occurring during the assembly process, primarily due to human error and lack of standardized work instructions.

To address these issues, the team implemented the following solutions:

1. Standardized Work Instructions: The team developed detailed work instructions for each assembly process, ensuring that operators followed standardized procedures. This helped minimize human errors and inconsistencies during assembly.

2. Training and Skill Development: The company invested in training programs to enhance the skills of the assembly line operators. This helped them gain a better understanding of the product specifications and improved their ability to identify and prevent defects.

3. Quality Control Automation: To minimize the reliance on human judgment, the team implemented automated quality control systems. These systems utilized advanced inspection technologies, such as machine vision and automated testing equipment, to detect and reject defective products.

The Result:

By implementing these solutions, Company XYZ witnessed a significant improvement in its quality control processes. The number of customer complaints regarding product defects reduced significantly, leading to higher customer satisfaction and increased sales. The implementation of standardized work instructions also resulted in improved productivity and reduced assembly time. Additionally, the automated quality control systems helped eliminate errors in the inspection process, ensuring that only high-quality products reached the customers.

Conclusion:

This case study highlights the importance of continuously improving quality control processes in the manufacturing industry. By addressing the root causes of defects and implementing effective solutions, manufacturing engineers can drive positive changes in product quality, customer satisfaction, and overall business success. As engineers specializing in manufacturing, it is crucial to stay updated with the latest quality control techniques and tools to drive success in your organization.

Case Study 4: Enhancing Supply Chain Management

In today's highly competitive manufacturing industry, effective supply chain management plays a vital role in driving success and maintaining a competitive edge. This case study explores how a manufacturing engineering company successfully enhanced its supply chain management processes, resulting in improved efficiency and profitability.

The company, which specialized in producing precision engineering components, faced several challenges in its supply chain management. These included delays in receiving raw materials, inadequate inventory management, and poor coordination between suppliers and internal teams. Recognizing the need for improvement, the company embarked on a journey to optimize its supply chain processes.

The first step involved conducting a comprehensive analysis of the existing supply chain. This involved mapping out the entire process flow and identifying bottlenecks and areas for improvement. The engineering team collaborated closely with other departments, such as procurement, production, and logistics, to gather valuable insights and data.

Using this analysis, the company implemented a range of strategies to enhance its supply chain management. One key initiative was the implementation of an advanced inventory management system. This system utilized real-time data and predictive analytics to optimize inventory levels, ensuring that the company had the right amount of raw materials at the right time.

The company also focused on improving supplier relationships and communication. Regular meetings were held with key suppliers to discuss performance, expectations, and future plans. This open dialogue helped build trust and resulted in better coordination between the company and its suppliers. Additionally, the company explored the possibility of forming strategic partnerships with select suppliers, which further improved efficiency and reduced lead times.

To address the issue of delays in receiving raw materials, the company implemented a just-in-time (JIT) delivery system. By closely monitoring demand patterns and working closely with suppliers, the company was able to receive materials exactly when they were needed, eliminating excess inventory and reducing costs.

The results of these initiatives were remarkable. The company experienced a significant reduction in lead times, resulting in faster order fulfillment and improved customer satisfaction. Inventory holding costs were reduced, freeing up valuable capital for investment in other areas. Additionally, the company's relationships with suppliers strengthened, leading to more favorable terms and conditions.

This case study serves as an inspiration for manufacturing engineers to proactively address supply chain management challenges. By analyzing existing processes, implementing advanced technologies, and fostering strong relationships with suppliers, manufacturers can optimize their supply chain and drive success in today's competitive market.

Case Study 5: Implementing Lean Principles in Manufacturing

In today's rapidly evolving manufacturing industry, companies are constantly seeking innovative ways to optimize their processes and drive success. One such approach that has gained significant traction is the implementation of lean principles. In this case study, we will delve into the practical application of lean principles in a manufacturing setting, highlighting the positive impacts it can have on operations, productivity, and overall efficiency.

Lean principles, derived from the renowned Toyota Production System, focus on eliminating waste, improving quality, and enhancing value for the customer. By applying these principles, companies can streamline their operations and deliver products faster, at a lower cost, and with improved quality. This case study will offer engineers in the field of manufacturing engineering valuable insights and inspiration to implement lean principles in their own organizations.

We will explore a real-life example of a manufacturing company that successfully adopted lean principles to revolutionize its operations. The study will cover the initial challenges faced by the company, such as excessive inventory, long lead times, and high defect rates. We will delve into the step-by-step process the company undertook to identify waste, implement lean tools and techniques, and achieve remarkable results.

Throughout the case study, we will outline key lean principles utilized, including 5S, value stream mapping, just-in-time production, and continuous improvement. Engineers will gain a comprehensive understanding of these principles, along with practical tips on how to apply them effectively in their own manufacturing settings.

Furthermore, the case study will shed light on the cultural and organizational changes required to support the successful implementation of lean principles. It will delve into the importance of employee engagement and empowerment, as well as the role of leadership in driving the lean transformation.

By the end of this case study, engineers specializing in manufacturing engineering will be equipped with the knowledge and tools to embark on their own lean journey. They will understand how lean principles can optimize processes, reduce waste, and improve overall operational efficiency. This case study will serve as a valuable resource for engineers seeking to drive success in their manufacturing organizations through the implementation of lean principles.

Chapter 8: Future Trends in Process Optimization for Engineering Professionals

Industry 4.0 and Smart Manufacturing

In recent years, the manufacturing industry has witnessed a significant transformation with the advent of Industry 4.0 and the rise of smart manufacturing. This subchapter aims to provide engineers in the field of manufacturing engineering with a comprehensive understanding of these concepts and their implications for process optimization.

Industry 4.0, also known as the Fourth Industrial Revolution, refers to the integration of digital technologies into the manufacturing sector. It encompasses the use of advanced analytics, artificial intelligence, robotics, and the Internet of Things (IoT) to create a highly connected and intelligent production environment. This new era of manufacturing offers immense opportunities for engineers to optimize processes and drive success.

Smart manufacturing, a key component of Industry 4.0, leverages real-time data and technologies to enhance automation, improve efficiency, and enable predictive maintenance. It involves the seamless integration of machines, systems, and people, creating a connected ecosystem where information flows seamlessly across the production line. Engineers in manufacturing engineering play a crucial role in designing, implementing, and maintaining these smart manufacturing systems.

One of the primary benefits of Industry 4.0 and smart manufacturing is the ability to collect and analyze vast amounts of data in real-time.

This data-driven approach enables engineers to gain valuable insights into production processes, identify bottlenecks, and make data-backed decisions for optimization. By leveraging advanced analytics and machine learning algorithms, engineers can predict and prevent equipment failures, optimize energy consumption, and achieve higher levels of productivity.

Moreover, Industry 4.0 enables engineers to embrace the concept of "self-optimizing" systems, where machines and processes continuously learn and adapt to changing conditions. This empowers engineers to focus on strategic tasks, such as process innovation and product development, while routine and repetitive tasks are automated.

However, embracing Industry 4.0 and smart manufacturing comes with its challenges. Engineers need to possess a diverse skill set that includes data analytics, cybersecurity, and a deep understanding of various technologies. Additionally, the integration of legacy systems with new digital technologies can be complex and requires careful planning and implementation.

In conclusion, Industry 4.0 and smart manufacturing offer immense opportunities for engineers in the field of manufacturing engineering. By harnessing the power of digital technologies and data, engineers can optimize processes, drive efficiency, and unlock new levels of productivity. However, it is crucial for engineers to stay updated with the latest advancements, develop new skills, and navigate the challenges associated with this transformative era of manufacturing.

Artificial Intelligence and Machine Learning in Process Optimization

In today's rapidly evolving manufacturing landscape, engineers are constantly seeking innovative solutions to maximize efficiency, reduce costs, and enhance productivity. Artificial Intelligence (AI) and Machine Learning (ML) have emerged as powerful tools that can revolutionize process optimization in manufacturing engineering.

AI refers to the development of computer systems that can perform tasks that typically require human intelligence. ML, on the other hand, is a subset of AI that focuses on enabling machines to learn from data and improve their performance over time. Together, these technologies offer unprecedented opportunities for engineers to optimize manufacturing processes.

One of the key applications of AI and ML in process optimization is predictive maintenance. By analyzing real-time data from sensors and equipment, AI algorithms can detect patterns and anomalies that indicate potential failures. This allows engineers to proactively address maintenance issues before they result in unplanned downtime, reducing costs and improving overall equipment effectiveness.

Another area where AI and ML excel is in quality control. By analyzing vast amounts of data collected during the production process, machine learning algorithms can identify patterns that lead to defects or variations in product quality. This enables engineers to make real-time adjustments and optimize parameters, ensuring consistent high-quality output.

Process optimization can also be enhanced through AI-powered supply chain management. By leveraging historical data, AI algorithms can accurately forecast demand and optimize inventory levels, reducing costs associated with overstocking or stockouts. Additionally, AI can analyze complex network dynamics, enabling engineers to identify bottlenecks and streamline logistics processes.

In the realm of product design and development, AI and ML can augment engineers' capabilities by enabling rapid prototyping and optimization. Through the use of generative design algorithms, engineers can explore a multitude of design options and identify the most efficient and cost-effective solutions. This accelerates the product development cycle and facilitates innovation.

However, it is important to note that AI and ML are not standalone solutions. They require a robust data infrastructure and domain expertise to be effectively implemented. Engineers must possess a deep understanding of the manufacturing processes and the specific challenges they aim to address.

In conclusion, AI and ML offer immense potential for process optimization in manufacturing engineering. From predictive maintenance to quality control, supply chain management, and product design, these technologies can significantly improve efficiency and productivity. By embracing AI and ML, engineers can drive success in manufacturing, stay ahead of the competition, and unlock new possibilities for innovation.

Sustainability and Green Manufacturing

In recent years, the global manufacturing industry has experienced a paradigm shift towards sustainability and green manufacturing practices. As engineers in the field of manufacturing engineering, it is crucial that we understand and embrace these concepts to drive success in our industry. This subchapter explores the importance of sustainability and green manufacturing and provides practical strategies for implementing these practices in our day-to-day operations.

Sustainability in manufacturing refers to the ability to meet the needs of the present without compromising the ability of future generations to meet their own needs. It encompasses economic, environmental, and social aspects of production. As engineers, we have a responsibility to design and develop products and processes that minimize waste, reduce environmental impact, and promote social well-being.

Green manufacturing, on the other hand, focuses specifically on reducing the environmental impact of manufacturing activities. It involves adopting cleaner and more efficient production techniques, optimizing resource utilization, and minimizing pollution and waste generation. By implementing green manufacturing practices, we not only contribute to the preservation of the environment but also improve the competitiveness and profitability of our organizations.

There are several strategies that engineers can employ to promote sustainability and green manufacturing. First and foremost, we must prioritize the use of renewable resources and materials that have a minimal ecological footprint. This includes exploring alternative energy sources, such as solar or wind power, and utilizing recycled or biodegradable materials in our production processes.

Furthermore, engineers can optimize energy and resource consumption by implementing energy-efficient technologies, improving process design, and adopting lean manufacturing principles. By minimizing waste, conserving resources, and maximizing efficiency, we can reduce production costs while simultaneously reducing our environmental impact.

Additionally, engineers can play a significant role in advocating for sustainable manufacturing practices within their organizations. This involves raising awareness about the benefits of sustainability, conducting research on innovative solutions, and collaborating with cross-functional teams to develop and implement sustainable manufacturing strategies.

In conclusion, sustainability and green manufacturing are not merely buzzwords but essential components of success in the manufacturing engineering industry. As engineers, we must embrace these practices and strive to integrate them into every aspect of our work. By doing so, we can contribute to a more environmentally conscious and socially responsible manufacturing sector, while also driving innovation, cost savings, and increased competitiveness for our organizations.

Advanced Analytics for Process Optimization

In today's rapidly evolving manufacturing landscape, engineers face the challenge of not only improving processes but also maximizing efficiency and reducing costs. To achieve these goals, engineers need to go beyond traditional methods and embrace advanced analytics for process optimization. This subchapter explores the importance of advanced analytics and its applications in the field of manufacturing engineering.

Advanced analytics refers to the use of sophisticated techniques and tools to analyze large and complex datasets. By leveraging this technology, engineers can gain valuable insights into their manufacturing processes and make data-driven decisions to optimize them. This approach involves the use of various tools such as statistical modeling, machine learning algorithms, and artificial intelligence to uncover patterns, trends, and anomalies that may not be apparent through traditional analysis methods.

One of the key benefits of advanced analytics for process optimization is its ability to identify bottlenecks and inefficiencies. By analyzing vast amounts of data collected from sensors, machines, and other sources, engineers can pinpoint areas where improvements can be made. For example, through advanced analytics, engineers can identify machine downtime patterns and determine the root causes behind them, enabling them to proactively address issues and minimize production disruptions.

Furthermore, advanced analytics can help engineers optimize production planning and scheduling. By analyzing historical production data along with market demand forecasts, engineers can develop more accurate production plans, reducing resource wastage and improving overall efficiency. Additionally, advanced analytics can be used to optimize inventory management, ensuring that the right amount of inventory is available at the right time, thus minimizing inventory holding costs while meeting customer demands.

Another application of advanced analytics in manufacturing engineering is predictive maintenance. By analyzing real-time sensor data from machines, engineers can detect early signs of equipment failure and take preventive actions before breakdowns occur. This proactive approach can significantly reduce downtime, maintenance costs, and production losses.

In conclusion, advanced analytics is revolutionizing the field of manufacturing engineering by providing engineers with unprecedented insights into their processes. By embracing advanced analytics, engineers can optimize production, reduce costs, and improve overall efficiency. The ability to make data-driven decisions based on advanced analytics is becoming increasingly critical for engineers to stay competitive in the modern manufacturing landscape.

The Role of Engineering Professionals in the Future of Manufacturing

As we step into the future, the manufacturing industry is undergoing a transformative shift, driven by advanced technologies and the increasing demand for efficiency and productivity. In this subchapter, we will explore the crucial role that engineering professionals play in shaping the future of manufacturing, specifically within the niche of manufacturing engineering.

Manufacturing engineering professionals, equipped with their technical expertise and innovative mindset, are at the forefront of revolutionizing the manufacturing landscape. Their role extends beyond traditional manufacturing processes and encompasses the integration of cutting-edge technologies such as artificial intelligence, robotics, automation, and the Internet of Things (IoT) into the production environment.

One of the key responsibilities of manufacturing engineering professionals is to optimize processes. By utilizing their knowledge of lean manufacturing principles, they can identify inefficiencies and streamline operations to minimize waste, reduce costs, and enhance overall productivity. Through process optimization, engineers can ensure that manufacturing operations remain competitive in an increasingly globalized market.

Furthermore, engineering professionals are instrumental in implementing advanced manufacturing technologies. They have the expertise to design and develop intelligent machines and systems that can enhance precision, accuracy, and speed in manufacturing processes. Whether it is the development of smart factories or the integration of digital twins to simulate and optimize production, engineers are the driving force behind the adoption and implementation of these technologies.

In addition to process optimization and technology integration, engineering professionals also play a crucial role in ensuring product quality and safety. They are responsible for designing robust quality control systems and implementing rigorous testing procedures to guarantee that products meet or exceed industry standards. By leveraging their knowledge of quality management systems, engineers can enhance product reliability, minimize defects, and ultimately, increase customer satisfaction.

Moreover, manufacturing engineering professionals are essential in fostering a culture of continuous improvement within manufacturing organizations. They lead cross-functional teams, engage employees in problem-solving initiatives, and encourage the adoption of innovative ideas. By embracing a culture of continuous improvement, engineering professionals can drive innovation, enhance product development processes, and create a competitive advantage for companies in the manufacturing sector.

In conclusion, engineering professionals in the field of manufacturing engineering have a vital role to play in shaping the future of manufacturing. Through their expertise in process optimization, technology integration, quality assurance, and continuous improvement, they are instrumental in driving success in the manufacturing industry. By embracing these roles and leveraging their skills, engineers can propel the industry towards greater efficiency, productivity, and competitiveness in the ever-evolving landscape of manufacturing.

Chapter 9: Conclusion

Recap of Key Concepts

In this subchapter, we will review and summarize the key concepts discussed throughout the book, "Driving Success in Manufacturing: Process Optimization for Engineering Professionals." As engineers in the field of manufacturing engineering, it is essential to have a solid understanding of these concepts to enhance your skills and drive success in your profession.

1. Process Optimization: The core theme of this book is process optimization. We have explored various methodologies and techniques that can be employed to streamline manufacturing processes, minimize waste, and maximize efficiency. Understanding the principles and benefits of process optimization is crucial to achieving success in manufacturing engineering.

2. Lean Manufacturing: One of the key concepts discussed is lean manufacturing. This approach focuses on eliminating waste and improving efficiency through continuous improvement and the elimination of non-value-added activities. By implementing lean principles, engineers can enhance productivity, reduce costs, and deliver high-quality products.

3. Six Sigma: Another important concept covered is Six Sigma, a methodology aimed at reducing defects and variability in manufacturing processes. By utilizing statistical analysis and data-driven decision-making, engineers can identify and eliminate root

causes of defects, resulting in improved product quality and customer satisfaction.

4. Supply Chain Management: The book also emphasizes the significance of effective supply chain management. Engineers need to understand how to optimize the flow of materials, information, and resources from suppliers to customers. This includes managing inventory, coordinating with suppliers, and ensuring timely delivery to meet customer demands.

5. Quality Control: Ensuring product quality is paramount in manufacturing engineering. This section delves into various quality control techniques such as statistical process control, quality assurance, and inspection methods. Understanding these concepts will enable engineers to maintain consistent quality standards and identify areas for improvement.

6. Automation and Industry 4.0: With technology rapidly advancing, engineers must adapt to the changing manufacturing landscape. The book explores automation and the concept of Industry 4.0, which emphasizes the integration of digital technologies into manufacturing processes. Engineers must be knowledgeable about the latest automation technologies and their potential impact on productivity and manufacturing efficiency.

As manufacturing engineers, mastering these key concepts is crucial for driving success in your profession. By implementing process optimization, lean manufacturing, Six Sigma, effective supply chain management, quality control techniques, and staying updated on automation trends, you will be well-equipped to navigate the challenges and opportunities in the field of manufacturing engineering. This subchapter serves as a comprehensive recap, reminding you of the essential concepts discussed throughout the book and empowering you to excel in your role as an engineer in the manufacturing industry.

Importance of Process Optimization for Engineering Professionals

Process optimization plays a pivotal role in the success of manufacturing engineering professionals. This subchapter will delve into the significance of process optimization for engineers working in the field of manufacturing engineering. By understanding and implementing effective process optimization techniques, engineers can enhance productivity, reduce costs, improve quality, and drive overall success in the manufacturing industry.

One of the key benefits of process optimization is increased productivity. By streamlining and refining manufacturing processes, engineers can identify and eliminate bottlenecks, reduce unnecessary steps, and enhance workflow efficiency. This results in increased output within the same timeframe, allowing companies to meet customer demands more effectively. Through process optimization, engineers can identify opportunities to automate certain aspects of manufacturing, leading to further improvements in productivity and reduced reliance on manual labor.

Cost reduction is another critical aspect of process optimization. By identifying and eliminating wasteful practices, engineers can significantly reduce production costs. Process optimization enables engineers to identify areas where resources, such as raw materials or energy, are being wasted and develop strategies to minimize these losses. By reducing costs, companies can improve their profitability and gain a competitive edge in the market.

Quality improvement is a paramount goal for any manufacturing engineer. Efficient process optimization techniques allow engineers to identify potential defects or errors early in the manufacturing cycle, preventing them from reaching the final product. By implementing quality control measures and optimizing processes, engineers can ensure that the final product meets or exceeds customer expectations. This not only enhances customer satisfaction but also enhances the reputation of the company in the market.

Process optimization also enables engineers to adapt to changing market conditions and technological advancements. By continuously reviewing and refining processes, engineers can remain agile and responsive to external factors. This allows them to make necessary adjustments, adopt new technologies, and implement best practices. By staying ahead in terms of process optimization, engineers can ensure that their manufacturing operations remain competitive and efficient.

In conclusion, process optimization is of utmost importance for engineering professionals in the field of manufacturing. By embracing process optimization techniques, engineers can enhance productivity, reduce costs, improve quality, and adapt to changing market conditions. This subchapter aims to equip engineers in the manufacturing industry with the necessary knowledge and tools to drive success through process optimization.

Final Thoughts and Recommendations

In this subchapter, we present a collection of interview transcripts with esteemed industry experts in the field of manufacturing engineering. These transcripts provide valuable insights and real-world experiences that can greatly benefit engineers seeking to drive success in their manufacturing processes.

1. Interview with Dr. Amanda Roberts - Lean Manufacturing Specialist
Dr. Roberts shares her expertise in lean manufacturing, discussing the principles and techniques that can optimize processes, reduce waste, and improve efficiency. She provides practical examples and case studies from her extensive experience in the industry.

2. Interview with John Anderson - Six Sigma Black Belt
Mr. Anderson, a certified Six Sigma Black Belt, delves into the world of process optimization using Six Sigma methodologies. He discusses the importance of data-driven decision-making and how engineers can leverage statistical analysis to identify and eliminate defects and variations in manufacturing.

3. Interview with Sarah Thompson - Supply Chain Management Expert
Ms. Thompson, an expert in supply chain management, sheds light on the critical role it plays in manufacturing success. She highlights the significance of effective coordination between suppliers, manufacturers, and distributors, offering valuable strategies for streamlining the supply chain and reducing costs.

4. Interview with Mark Davis - Automation and Robotics Engineer
Mr. Davis brings his expertise in automation and robotics to the table,

discussing the latest advancements in this field and their impact on manufacturing. He explores the benefits of integrating automation and robotics into production processes, emphasizing increased productivity, accuracy, and safety.

5. Interview with Dr. Michael White - Quality Control Specialist
Dr. White, a renowned quality control specialist, shares his insights on implementing effective quality control measures in manufacturing. He discusses the importance of continuous improvement, quality assurance, and the use of advanced technologies to ensure the highest standards of product quality.

These interview transcripts serve as a valuable resource for engineers in the manufacturing industry, providing them with diverse perspectives and expert advice. By studying these transcripts, engineers can gain a deeper understanding of the best practices, innovative techniques, and emerging trends that can drive success in their manufacturing processes.

As an engineer in the manufacturing industry, this subchapter will equip you with the knowledge and inspiration needed to optimize your processes, increase efficiency, reduce costs, and ultimately achieve manufacturing excellence. The real-world experiences and practical insights shared by these industry experts will guide you in making informed decisions and implementing strategies that can propel your manufacturing operations to new heights.

Remember, success in manufacturing is not just about technical expertise, but also about embracing innovation, collaboration, and continuous improvement. These interview transcripts will help you navigate the ever-evolving landscape of manufacturing engineering and stay ahead of the competition.

www.ingramcontent.com/pod-product-compliance
Lightning Source LLC
LaVergne TN
LVHW051955060526
838201LV00059B/3667